Learning Through Literacy

*Adapting Novels By Roald Dahl
For Students in Self-Contained
or Inclusive Classrooms*

By Kathleen Brady
and Eileen Phelan

Cataloging-in-Publication Data

Brady, Kathleen, 1973-
  Learning through literacy : adapting novels by Roald Dahl for students in self-contained or inclusive classrooms / by Kathleen Brady and Eileen Phelan.
      p. cm. -- (The professional growth series)
   Includes bibliographical references and index.
      ISBN 1-58683-010-4 (perfect bound)
     1. Dahl, Roald--Study and teaching (Elementary) 2. Dahl, Roald--Adaptations--Study and teaching (Elementary) 3. Children's stories, English--Study and teaching (Elementary) 4. Children's stories, English--Adaptations--Study and teaching (Elementary) 5. Special education--Activity programs. 6. Literacy programs. I. Phelan, Eileen, 1973- II. Title. III. Series.

PR6054.A35 Z53 2001
371.9'0444—dc21

2001037725

Published by Linworth Publishing, Inc.
480 East Wilson Bridge Road, Suite L
Worthington, Ohio 43085

Copyright © 2002 by Linworth Publishing, Inc.

Series Information:
    From The Professional Growth Series

All rights reserved. Reproduction of this book in whole or in part is prohibited without written permission of the author.

1-58683-010-4

5 4 3 2 1

Table of Contents

Introduction iv
    Objectives iv
    Applications iv
    Features iv
    How to Use This Book v
Bloom's Taxonomy v
Adapting Literature Instruction vi
    Adapting Instructional Presentation vi
    Adapting Instructional Directions vii
    Motivational Methods vii
    Reinforcement Activities vii
Tips for Teaching Listening and Note-Taking Skills .viii
    Listening Skills ix
    Note-Taking Skills x
Rubrics xi
    What Is a Rubric? xi
    What to Look for When Using a Rubric xi
Roald Dahl Biography xiii
References xiii
Story Summaries xiv
The Magic Finger 1
Fantastic Mr. Fox 22
The Twits 42
George's Marvelous Medicine 62
The Witches 82
Appendix 102

Introduction

Objectives

This book is designed to enable special education students to extend their appreciation of quality, grade-appropriate literature while they develop their higher-level thinking skills. It is intended for use in a broader, multisensory communication arts program. The activities in this book are offered as ways to help special education students in grades 3–5 meet the content standards produced by the National Council of Teachers of English and the International Reading Association (1996).

The objectives of this book are as follows:
1. To provide the adaptations and modifications necessary for special education students to engage in grade-appropriate literature.
2. To develop within students higher-level critical thinking skills.
3. To provide students with practice in test taking and to assist teachers with introducing test-taking strategies as part of their communication arts program.
4. To provide students with the opportunity to read and comprehend several books by one author.
5. To develop within students effective ways of talking and writing about literature they have read.

Applications

This book is a companion to books written by Roald Dahl. Students in grades 3–5 will thoroughly enjoy reading these books and the activities that accompany them. In addition to imaginative teaching aids to encourage the development of critical thinking skills, there are sections devoted to increasing vocabulary through fun instructional games, phonics elements, and language skills reinforcement.

While this book is aimed at providing learning disabled students with the opportunity to read and enjoy grade-appropriate literature, the activities in this book can be adapted to almost any classroom setting. A special program's population is varied and requires individualization, and the tips provided in this book lend themselves nicely to small reading groups, independent reading activities, Resource Room or Title 1 settings.

Features

- **Bloom's Taxonomy:** This section provides an explanation of Bloom's Taxonomy of Educational Objectives and how it relates to the activities within this book.
- **Adapting Literature Instruction:** This section provides an overview of modifications that aid effective and efficient instruction. It includes instructional presentations that ensure student learning, methods of explaining the directions, motivational activities that encourage student involvement, and reinforcement activities for faster successful learning experiences.
- **Tips for Teaching Listening and Note-Taking Skills:** This section offers strategies to foster listening and note-taking skills in your students, accompanied by worksheets to organize the information.
- **Novel Tie-Ins:** For each book presented, phonics elements, vocabulary words, and a language skill have been highlighted.
- **Author Study:** An overview of the life of Roald Dahl is presented along with a short synopsis of each novel covered in this book.

- **Critical Thinking Activity Sheets:** Based upon Bloom's Taxonomy (1956), activity sheets are provided to be used in conjunction with each book.
- **Test-taking Strategy:** Along with each book, a test-taking strategy is presented, and a sample lesson is provided.
- **Cumulative Test:** New, tougher standards are being implemented across the country that will determine the promotion of students in both general and special education classes. Following the standardized format, a cumulative test has been included to accompany each book in order to provide the students with vital practice in taking tests.
- **Appendix:** At the end of the book is an appendix containing graphic organizers that can be used by teachers to develop their students' writing skills.

How to Use This Book

We wrote this book because as special education classroom teachers we felt that we often were forced to choose between using literature that was instructionally appropriate but emotionally immature for our students or spending many hours creating our own material to adapt grade-appropriate literature to meet our students' needs. Special education teachers, general education classroom teachers, and media specialists can use the activities contained within this book to foster a love of reading in their students and improve their comprehension skills. As teachers, we know that change, flexibility, and individualization are integral parts of daily instruction. We hope that the activities contained within this book serve as an important component of your broader reading program.

Bloom's Taxonomy

Difficulties with decoding written language are not the only problems facing students with learning disabilities when they read. Retelling and comprehending what they have read also is challenging for many students. The activities in this book were designed to increase the students' ability to retell facts and information and to develop the students' critical thinking skills. We chose the objectives from Bloom's Taxonomy as a framework because they clearly outline the skills necessary to process and manipulate information.

- **Knowledge:** This objective involves the basic recall of information.
  Example: Retelling events from a story
- **Comprehension:** When we ask students a comprehension question, we are asking them to *interpret* or *redefine* information they have processed.
  Example: Telling why an event happened
- **Application:** This is a *problem-solving* objective.
  Example: Telling what a character should do to resolve a conflict
- **Analysis:** This objective involves *breaking down* information.
  Example: Identifying elements within a story
- **Synthesis:** This objective is the opposite of analysis. It involves *creating* or *designing* something new based upon the information already processed.
  Example: Creating a new ending for a story
- **Evaluation:** This is the highest-level critical thinking skill. It involves *forming opinions* or *making judgments*.
  Example: Telling who your favorite character in a book is and explaining why

Adapting Literature Instruction

This section is devoted to providing useful strategies for teachers to adapt the novels to meet the varied needs of special education students.

Adapting Instructional Presentation

Students with learning disabilities have individual needs and differences. It is therefore necessary to vary the mode of presentation, conceptual development, format, and length of each lesson.

- Students who are reading at or above grade level may enjoy reading independently, with follow-up and guidance from the teacher. Have the student complete a daily reading log to mark his or her progress through the book. This method has proven successful with students with emotional or behavioral disabilities as it builds responsibility and a sense of independence and accomplishment within the students.
- Provide chapters on audiocassette for those students having difficulty decoding. Many publishing companies allow tapes to be made of excerpts of their books for classroom use. You also can purchase books on tape from many educational publishing companies. This allows students the opportunity to improve their critical thinking and listening comprehension skills. For the same reasons, include opportunities for read-alouds during your presentations of each book.
- Guided reading groups should include advance support. Always review the students' prior knowledge of the book. Encourage students to make predictions about what will happen next. Allow them to use illustrations before they read in order to create meaning out of what they are reading.
- For students with visual perception difficulties, copy and enlarge the print to make it more clear. You also can provide them with an easy-to-make "reading frame" that limits the amount of text they can see on the page.
- Break down the amount of text your students read at any given time. Stop frequently and discuss what they have read. If the students' responses indicate they are not constructing meaning appropriate to what they have read, redirect them as needed before continuing.
- Introduce vocabulary before the students read each section. Let the students become familiar enough with the vocabulary that they will recognize the word when reading and will understand it in context.
- Limit the number of extension activities assigned to each student based on their abilities. For some students, you may want to cut a page in half and assign each half separately (i.e., class work/homework).
- We have included different methods of responses, such as drawing and writing, in the extension activities. Some students also may find it necessary to tape record answers, respond orally, or have their answers scribed.
- Utilize different methods of presentation for all the students. Children love variety as much as adults. Not only will this keep them interested in each book, but it also will allow them to access their different strengths as auditory, visual, or kinesthetic learners.

Adapting Instructional Directions

When creating this book, we made the directions clear and simple. The following suggestions will enhance student understanding of what is expected of them during any lesson.

- Ask students to orally repeat the directions given by the teacher before beginning any activity.
- When the students read the directions themselves, ask them to repeat what they are going to do.
- If a student is confused about the directions, let another student explain the directions and have the first student repeat them.

Motivational Methods

Motivating students to learn is a key element in any successful reading program. Due to the fear of failure that many special education students experience, it is especially important that we keep their interest and allow them to become engaged in their reading material. We chose these books by Roald Dahl because we have found them to be highly interesting and entertaining to our students. The following strategies will contribute to student motivation.

- Provide a safe learning environment. It is absolutely necessary that students know that they will not face ridicule from their classmates or admonishment from their teacher for making mistakes.
- Allow the students choice concerning the methods of reading the material.
- Utilize the students' background as a way to help them relate to the story they are reading.

Reinforcement Activities

Learning centers can be an important tool for providing students with learning disabilities with the necessary opportunities to master an instructional objective. The following learning center activities are designed to increase the amount and types of reinforcements available to your students.

- Provide audiotapes of the chapters currently being read available at your listening center. You also may want to have questions about the book on tape. Students can listen and then answer at their own pace.
- Utilize your computer center for response writing about the book. Students can type their writing in a large-size font, print their work, and then read it to a classmate or the teacher.
- File folders make great activities for phonics or vocabulary centers. Simply choose a skill that you feel needs reinforcement, create an activity to reinforce that skill, attach it to a file folder, and cover with contact paper. Keep the folders in a place students have access to. Students can get the folders and work independently, and you can keep the folders for years.
- Create a "team center." In this center, classmates can assist students who are having difficulty.

Tips for Teaching Listening and Note-Taking Skills

Aim: How do we take notes?

Objectives
1. Students will practice active listening skills.
2. Students will identify relevant information when listening to a passage.
3. Students will learn different ways of organizing their notes.

Procedures
These activities are designed to be part of ongoing instruction, not one isolated lesson.

- Strengthen the students' listening skills. Hand out Worksheet A and reinforce the behaviors listed. Make sure the students internalize these behaviors. Discuss correct listening behaviors daily.

- Start with read-alouds of short passages (as short as one sentence if necessary). Have the students visualize what they hear and then have them repeat back what they heard. Build up to longer passages as students' listening skills become stronger.

- Let the students draw a picture describing what you have read to them.

- Hand out Worksheet B. Frequently review the information on it with students.

- Teach the students to listen for important information (names, places, action words).

- Begin note-taking lessons by using a graphic organizer. Effective organizers are Venn diagrams, sequence maps, or story maps. Use an overhead projector to model how you fill in the information.

- Introduce the outline format by modeling to students how to list information.

- Some students will not be able to take notes. Provide a scribe for these students if possible. Teaching them to organize and classify information is still beneficial to their recall of information.

- Frequently assess for mastery.

- Reteaching and reviewing will be necessary. This is a difficult skill for many students in special education.

Worksheet A

Listening and Note-Taking Skills

Part 1: Listening Skills

Listening is one of the most important skills you can have in school. If you have good listening skills, you can be more successful in all your school subjects.

- **Look** at the person who is speaking. It will help you to focus on what the person is saying.

- **Stay Quiet!** You cannot listen if you are talking.

- **Concentrate!** Try to focus on what you are listening to. Remember there is a difference between hearing and listening. You don't want to let information "go in one ear and out the other."

- **Make a movie** in your mind. If you can picture in your mind what you are listening to, you will be able to remember it better.

- **Be a detective** and listen for clues. If you hear a name, place, or event repeated, it's probably important.

- **Pay attention** to your teacher's body language. Is he or she leaning forward, looking around, or reading some parts of the story very clearly or slowly? These are probably important parts.

Listening and Note-Taking Skills

Part 2: Note-Taking Skills

Taking notes doesn't mean writing down every word you hear. It means writing down only the most important points.

- **Use your listening skills!** If you pay close attention to what you have read, it will be easier to decide what you should write down.

- **DO NOT** try to write every word. Use abbreviations.

- **DO NOT** write in full sentences.

- **DO NOT** worry about spelling.

- **Leave out words** such as *and*, *the*, and *an*.

- **Organize your paper** into an outline or map format.

- **If something is repeated**, it is probably important. Write it down!

Rubrics

What Is a Rubric?

Rubrics are guidelines that define standards of writing. Rubrics are used to provide clear and detailed explanations as to what is required of a writing task. It gives the teacher and the students a point of reference whereby specific areas of strengths and weaknesses in writing can be identified with greater clarity. The use of rubrics for evaluation purposes allows for more standardized grading. The rubric included in this book is used to evaluate writing that is in response to questions about the text. It consists of a 4 to 1 grading scale that defines each level of writing.

What to Look for When Using a Rubric

4 Response A 4 response demonstrates a thorough understanding of the question. A 4 response must give an awareness of purpose in the writing. The student must present a clear point of view, showing focus and expansion upon a main idea. It must be organized with a beginning, middle, and end while having a clear introduction and a concluding sentence. Details and examples from the text, which provide support for main ideas, should be apparent. Word choices should be grade appropriate, and adjectives and adverbs should be used to enhance the response. All or most words should be spelled correctly, and sentences should have proper punctuation.

3 Response The overall development of the response is moderately clear but may include some inaccuracies. The response is somewhat organized but may not have an introduction or closure. Details should be included in most of the response. Sentences should be coherent and complex. While expressions of thought may be more limited, age-appropriate vocabulary should be used. The spelling of words and the use of punctuation should be mostly correct.

2 Response A 2 response shows limited understanding and an overall lack of cohesion. It is written with a minimal number of sentences but shows some order. A topic sentence related to the main idea is evident, but supporting details may not be present. The sentences are relatively simple, each representing one thought. While word choices may not be age appropriate, some vocabulary relates to the topic. The response includes both inventive and common spelling.

1 Response The 1 response is not developed and shows no understanding or sense of purpose. There is no organization or logical order. The response may include pictures that relate to the main idea. Sentences may consist of illogical fragments or may be nonexistent. The vocabulary is extremely limited, and groups of letters may be combined to represent words.

We have included a sample rubric on the following page for use when evaluating your students' written work.

	Overall Development	Organization	Supportive Details	Sentence Structure	Word Choice	Mechanics
4	Aware of Purpose	• has a beginning, middle and end • sequences events • has introduction and closure	• given a topic, can produce a topic sentence and appropriate details • uses pronouns to replace nouns	• uses varied types of sentences	• uses adjectives and adverbs to enhance writing	• Spells almost all words correctly • uses all punctuation correctly
3	Moderately clear	• has a beginning, middle and end • no introduction or closure	• given a topic, can produce several detail sentences	• can create more complex sentences, e.g., compound subjects or predicates	• limited use of descriptive language	• spells most common words correctly • uses a variety of end punctuation
2	Lacking cohesion	• can write 2–3 sentences in logical order	• can write a sentence related to the main idea	• each written sentence represents one thought	• uses vocabulary that relates to the topic	• uses both inventive and common spelling
1	Not developed	• no sense of organization or sequence	• can draw a picture that relates to the main idea	• creates writing that sounds like "talk"	• extremely limited vocabulary	• uses groups of letters to represent words • leaves spaces between "words"

Roald Dahl Biography

Roald Dahl was born in Wales in 1916. He was educated at a British boarding school. He had very unhappy experiences while a student there, which are reflected in his later stories and novels. As a young adult, Dahl joined the Shell Oil Company, hoping to travel the world and find adventure. He did indeed travel to Africa, learn Swahili and contract malaria. At the start of World War II, Dahl enlisted in the Royal Air Force (RAF) and served as a fighter pilot and air attaché in Washington, DC. During those years, he began his career as a published writer, producing RAF adventure stories for the *Saturday Evening Post* and his first novel, *The Gremlins* (1943), which became a movie in 1984.

Roald Dahl continued to write successful adult fiction. However, he is best known as the best-selling author of 19 children's books. *James and the Giant Peach* (1961), *Charlie and the Chocolate Factory* (1964), and *Matilda* (1988) are just a few of his well-known works. He also wrote a number of film scripts including *You Only Live Twice* (1967) and *Chitty Chitty Bang Bang* (1968).

Dahl wrote two autobiographies, *Boy* (1984) and *Going Solo* (1986). He was married for 30 years to American actress Patricia Neal. Unfortunately it was not a happy marriage. No children survived, and Patricia suffered a series of severe strokes, with Dahl nursing her back to health. They divorced in 1983.

Roald Dahl quickly married Felicity Dahl, with whom he had been carrying on an affair for many years. This was a happy and productive time in Dahl's life. He continued writing until he died in 1990.

References

Roald Dahl
http:// www.roalddahlfans.com
http: // www.encarta.msn.com

For more information about Roald Dahl, or to locate other activities to use with his books, the following Web sites are excellent.
http://www.geocities.com/Hollywood/Academy.4613
http://tqjunior.advanced.org/5113
http:// falcon.jmu.edu/~ramseyil/dahl.htm

Other References
Bloom, B.S., M.B. Engelhart, S.J. Furst, W.H. Hill, and D.R. Krathwohl. *Taxonomy Of Educational Objectives. The Classification of Educational Goals. Handbook I: Cognitive Domain.* New York: Longmans Green, 1956.

National Council Of Teachers of English & International Reading Association. *Standards For the English Language Arts.* Urbana, IL and Newark, DE: NCTE and IRA, 1996.

Story Summaries

The Magic Finger
The Greggs are a family that likes nothing better than to hunt animals for fun. This all changes when the girl next door gets angry and puts the Magic Finger on them. When they wake up the next day, they are bird-sized, with wings instead of arms! This is just the beginning of their problems. When they have to build their own nest because human-sized birds have moved into their home, the Greggs' attitude about hunting begins to change.

Fantastic Mr. Fox
Mr. Fox is the head of the Fox family. All he wants to do is find enough food to feed his wife and children. Unfortunately, Mr. Fox has to outwit a criminal team of farmers who are determined to destroy the entire Fox family! They have the Foxes trapped inside their den with nothing to eat. Mr. Fox has to come up with a very risky plan in order to save his family.

The Twits
No one has ever met anyone as horrible as Mr. and Mrs. Twit! They spend their lives playing mean tricks on each other and being nasty to each other. When they capture Muggle-Wump the monkey, he decides that in order to win his freedom, he must play a trick on the Twits!

George's Marvelous Medicine
George is a little boy with a problem. He has been left alone with his terrible old Grandma, who might be a witch. After being threatened, yelled at, and scared by Grandma, George decides to take action. He concocts a medicine that will cure Grandma of her nastiness. When George finally feeds Grandma the medicine, the results are marvelous!

The Witches
A young boy on vacation with his Grandma accidentally overhears a conference between all the witches of England and the Grand High Witch of all the world! They have a plan to destroy all the children of England, but luckily, this little boy's Grandma knows something about witches. Together they try to stop the witches from acting out their evil plan.

Reprinted by permission of the Estate of Roald Dahl and the Watkins/Loomis Agency.

The Magic Finger

Key Vocabulary

hunting	whiskers	cross
wild	robins	enormous
nest	surprise	woods
queer	hammer	

Vocabulary Instruction
Introduce the selected vocabulary words. Model the correct pronunciation, and elicit the meanings of each word. Have the students illustrate a "Magic Finger Vocabulary Book." On each page of the book, the students will illustrate the meaning of a vocabulary word. The students may keep the books in their desks and refer to them when necessary.

Focus On Phonics

Digraphs: ch, sh, th, wh   **Short Vowel Sounds**

Sample Word List

Consonant Digraphs
she	what
thin	shout
nothing	where
catch	both
witches	

Short Vowel Words
duck	nest
Gregg	ten
can	tell
class	hit
thin	

Language Skills

Parts of Speech: Classifying words as nouns or verbs
See Language Skills Activity Sheet on page 14.

The Magic Finger   **Knowledge 1**

Name_____ Date_____

What's What?

Directions: Answer the following questions in complete sentences. Remember to CAPITALIZE the first letter and use a period at the end of your sentence.

What were Mr. Gregg, Phillip and William doing when the little girl put the magic finger on them?

_____

_____

What did the ducks do that surprised the Greggs?

_____

_____

What happened to the Greggs when they woke up in the morning?

_____

_____

Draw a picture of the Gregg family after they woke up in the morning.

The Magic Finger Knowledge 2

Name_____ Date_____

Mixed-Up Ducks

Directions: Answer the following questions using complete sentences. Remember to CAPITALIZE the first letter and use a period at the end of your sentence.

How did the magic finger change the ducks?

_____

_____

_____

_____

What did the Greggs do after the ducks moved into their house?

_____

_____

_____

_____

What did the ducks do inside the Greggs' house?

_____

_____

_____

_____

The Magic Finger　　　　　　　　　　　　　　　　　　　　**Comprehension 1**

Name_____ Date_____

Feelings

Directions: Explain how Mr. Gregg felt at the beginning, middle and end of the story. Illustrate your answers in the boxes.

Beginning: Mr. Gregg felt _____ because
_____

Middle: Mr. Gregg felt _____ because
_____

End: Mr. Gregg felt _____ because
_____

Learning Through Literacy

The Magic Finger Comprehension 2

Name_____ Date_____

All Mixed Up

Directions: Put a number next to each sentence to retell the story in order.

Mr. Gregg changed his name to Egg.   _____

The Gregg family went hunting.   _____

The ducks followed the Greggs home.   _____

The little girl used her magic finger.   _____

The Greggs grew wings.   _____

The Greggs moved into the nest.   _____

The little girl went to find the Coopers.   _____

The Magic Finger　　　　　　　　　　　　　　　　　　　　**Application 1**

Name_____ Date_____

Mix- Up

Directions: Draw a picture of a person in Box A and write his or her name on the line below. Draw a picture of an animal in Box B and write its name on the line below.

A	**B**

_____　　　_____

List three characteristics of a person.　　　List three characteristics of an animal.

　1. _____　　　1. _____

　2. _____　　　2. _____

　3. _____　　　3. _____

How are a person and an animal the same?

_____

How are a person and an animal different?

_____

6 Learning Through Literacy

The Magic Finger Application 2

Name_____ Date_____

How Did They Change?

Directions: In the boxes below, identify three changes that happened to the characters in the story that were caused by the magic finger.

[ ] [ ] [ ]

Explain how the changes helped or hurt the characters.

_____
_____
_____
_____
_____
_____
_____

The Magic Finger   Analysis 1

Name_____ Date_____

Fact or Fantasy

Directions: Read the sentences. Write FACT next to the sentence if that could happen in real life. Write FANTASY if the sentence could not happen in real life.

1. _____ A teacher can grow a tail.

2. _____ People hunt for ducks for fun.

3. _____ Some people grow wings.

4. _____ Ducks live in nests.

5. _____ A finger has magic powers.

6. _____ People grow whiskers.

7. _____ Some people have ducks as pets.

8. _____ People change their names.

9. _____ Ducks have babies.

10. _____ People get to fly to other places.

Draw a picture of a fact (something that can happen in real life) and a fantasy (something that cannot happen in real life).

FACT   **FANTASY**

Learning Through Literacy

The Magic Finger　　　　　　　　　　　　　　　　　　　　Analysis 2

Name_____ Date_____

Compare and Contrast

Directions: Using the diagram below, compare and contrast the ducks and the Greggs.

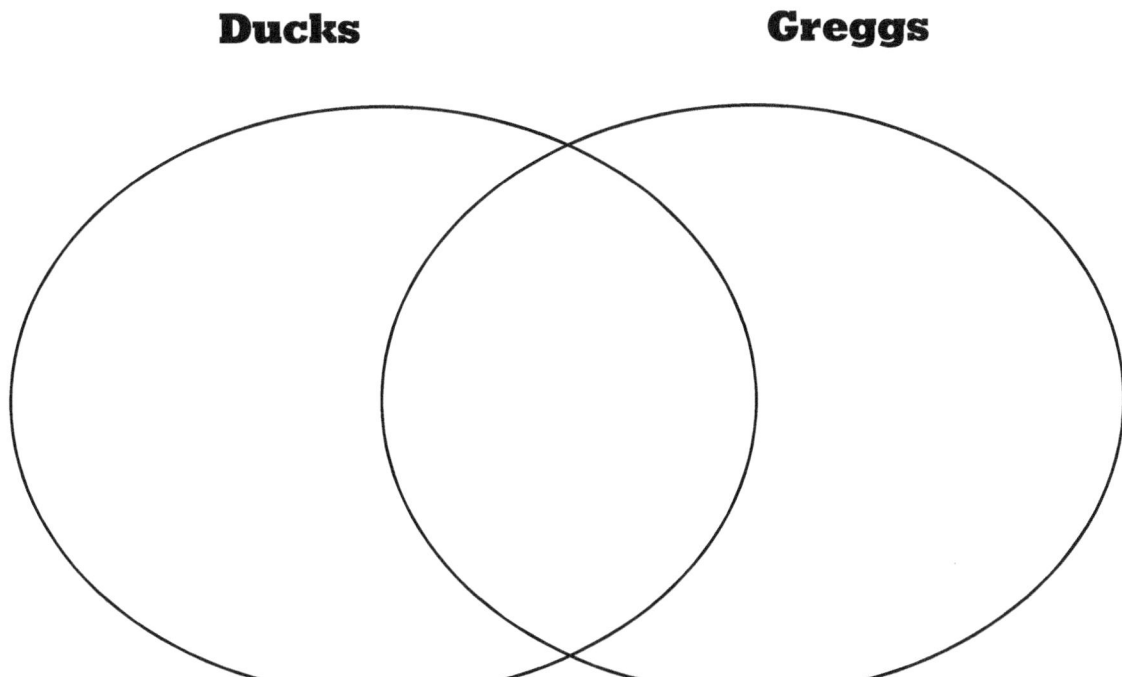

How are the ducks and the Greggs similar?

_____

_____

_____

How are the ducks and the Greggs different?

_____

_____

_____

The Magic Finger Synthesis 1

Name_____ Date_____

Wacky Creatures

Directions: In the story *The Magic Finger*, Mrs. Winter grew cat whiskers. The Gregg family grew wings. The ducks grew arms. Pick an animal from the box below. Create your own creature by combining the characteristics of an animal with a person.

dog	fish	elephant	alligator
rabbit	zebra	horse	lion

Write five sentences that describe your new creature.

_____

_____

_____

_____

_____

Draw a picture of your creature.

The Magic Finger   Synthesis 2

Name_____ Date_____

Helping Hands

Directions: In the book *The Magic Finger*, the Greggs could not eat an apple because of their wings. Imagine having wings instead of hands. In the boxes below, list things you could do with wings and things you could not do with wings.

THINGS YOU **CAN** DO WITH WINGS	THINGS YOU **CAN'T** DO WITH WINGS
_____	_____
_____	_____
_____	_____
_____	_____
_____	_____

Write a paragraph about some of the things you could not do if you had wings instead of hands.

_____
_____
_____
_____
_____
_____
_____

The Magic Finger   **Evaluation 1**

Name_____ Date_____

Open Ballot

Directions: In the story, the little girl becomes angry at the Greggs because they went hunting for ducks. Do you agree with the little girl? Check one of the boxes to cast your vote.

☐ I think hunting ducks for fun **should** be allowed.

☐ I think hunting ducks for fun **should not** be allowed.

Write a letter to a friend. Explain why you voted this way. Try to convince your friend that you are right.

                         Date_____

Dear_____ ,

_____

_____

_____

_____

_____

_____

_____

_____

                                 Yours truly,

                                 _____

The Magic Finger   **Evaluation 2**

Name _____   Date _____

Book Critique

Directions: Pretend you are a book critic. Fill out the form below. Write a recommendation as to why the book should be read or not.

Name of Book _____

Author of Book _____

Classification (mark an X)

☐ Biography   ☐ How to   ☐ Fantasy

☐ Fable   ☐ Mystery   ☐ Science Fiction

Characters

_____   _____

_____   _____

What was the book about?

_____

_____

I would rate this book (circle one):

☆poor   ☆☆fair   ☆☆☆good   ☆☆☆☆excellent

I rated it _____ because _____

_____

Signature _____   Date _____

The Magic Finger **Language Skills**

Name_____ Date_____

Identifying Nouns And Verbs

Nouns are words that name a person, place or thing.
   Examples: boy, forest, glass

Verbs are words that tell what someone or something is doing.
   Examples: running, laugh, yell

Directions: Circle the nouns in each sentence below. Underline the verbs in each sentence below.

Mrs. Winter was laughing at the little girl.

The little girl came running over.

The Greggs went hunting.

They began shooting at the ducks in the forest.

The ducks flew away.

Mr. Gregg woke up.

Mrs. Gregg was still sleeping.

The ducks moved into their house.

The Greggs built a nest in a tree.

The little girl pointed her finger.

Test-Taking Skills 1

Following Directions

Aim: Why is following directions important when you are taking a test?

Objectives
1. The students will become familiar with test vocabulary.
2. The students will listen to and read test directions.

Procedures
These activities are designed to be part of ongoing instruction, not one isolated lesson.

- Introduce vocabulary that the students will encounter on tests. Example should include: *STOP, GO ON, opposite, same, choose, locate, read, write, paragraph, selection, respond, underline*. Discuss the meanings of all these words. Include these words in other classroom activities.

- Tell the class when you are about to give them directions. Include test vocabulary in your daily classroom directions. For example, say:
  - I'm going to give you directions on the count of five. 1, 2, 3, 4, 5.
  - Open your science books to page 85. Read the title.
  - Now put your finger on the beginning of the first paragraph.

Make sure that the students understand each simple direction before continuing.

- Provide the students with activities that have written directions. Let them read the directions themselves without providing oral directions.

- On classroom assignments and teacher-made tests, give the students different types of test directions.

- Assess the extent to which the students have mastered this skill. Provide feedback and additional support as necessary.

The Magic Finger **Sample Test**

Name_____ Date_____

Sample Test, Part 1

Directions: Read the selection from *The Magic Finger*. Then answer questions 1–7.

For months I had been telling myself that I would never put the Magic Finger on anyone again—not after what happened to my teacher, old Mrs. Winter.

Poor Mrs. Winter.

One day we were in class, and she was teaching us spelling. "Stand up," she said to me, "and spell cat."

"That's an easy one." I said. "K-A-T."

"You are a stupid little girl!"

"I am not a stupid little girl!" I cried. "I am a very nice little girl!"

"Go and stand in the corner," Mrs. Winter said.

Then I got cross*, and I saw red, and I put the Magic Finger on Mrs. Winter good and strong, and almost at once…

Guess what?

Whiskers began growing out of her face! They were long black whiskers, just like the ones you see on a cat, only much bigger. And how fast they grew!

Before we had time to think, they were out to her ears!

Of course the whole class started screaming with laughter, and then Mrs. Winter said, "Will you be so kind as to tell me what you find so madly funny, all of you?"

And when she turned around to write something on the blackboard we saw that she had grown a tail as well! It was a huge bushy tail!

I cannot begin to tell you what happened after that, but if any of you are wondering whether Mrs. Winter is quite all right now, the answer is No. And she never will be.

The Magic Finger is something I have been able to do all my life. I can't tell you how I do it, because I don't even know myself. But it always happens when I get cross*, when I see red…

Cross—angry or mad

The Magic Finger **Sample Test**

Name_____ Date_____

1. What is this selection mostly about?
   A. A girl who gets in trouble at school
   B. A class of bad children
   C. A teacher changed by magic
   D. A girl who can't spell

2. Mrs. Winter calls the little girl "stupid" because
   A. she added wrong.
   B. she hit another student.
   C. she grew a tail.
   D. she spelled a word wrong.

3. The next time the girl spells a word wrong, Mrs. Winter will most likely
   A. send her to the principal.
   B. help her to spell it.
   C. call her stupid.
   D. send her to the corner.

4. The girl's finger begins to tingle when
   A. she is happy.
   B. she is excited.
   C. she is angry.
   D. she is sad.

5. When strange things began to happen to Mrs. Winter, the students
   A. became frightened.
   B. started to cry.
   C. laughed.
   D. ran from the room.

6. Which word best describes Mrs. Winter?
   A. kind
   B. mean
   C. happy
   D. funny

7. Which of the following could not happen in real life?
   A. A little girl gets angry.
   B. A teacher writes on the blackboard.
   C. A teacher grows a tail.
   D. Students scream with laughter.

The Magic Finger 17

The Magic Finger Sample Test

Name_____ Date_____

Sample Test, Part 2

Directions: You are going to listen to a selection from *The Magic Finger*. You will answer two questions about the chapter.

Listen to the chapter twice. The first time you hear the chapter, listen carefully. The second time you hear it, take notes on what you hear. Then use your notes to help you answer the questions.

_____ NOTES _____

The Magic Finger **Sample Test**

Name_____ Date_____

1. **Read** the two quotations from the story below. **Explain** how the characters felt when they said this. Why did they feel this way?

   Mrs. Gregg began to cry. "Oh dear! Oh dear!" she sobbed. "They have taken our house. What shall we do? We have no place to go!"

   Feeling— _____
   _____
   _____
   _____

   "How warm it is!" said William. "And what fun to be living so high up," said Phillip. "We may be small, but nobody can hurt us up here."

   Feeling— _____
   _____
   _____
   _____

2. Explain why the Greggs didn't understand the ducks' feelings until they grew wings and lived in a nest.

   _____
   _____
   _____
   _____

The Magic Finger **Sample Test**

Name_____ Date_____

Sample Test, Part 3

Directions: Use details from the story to show the difference between living in a house and living in a nest.

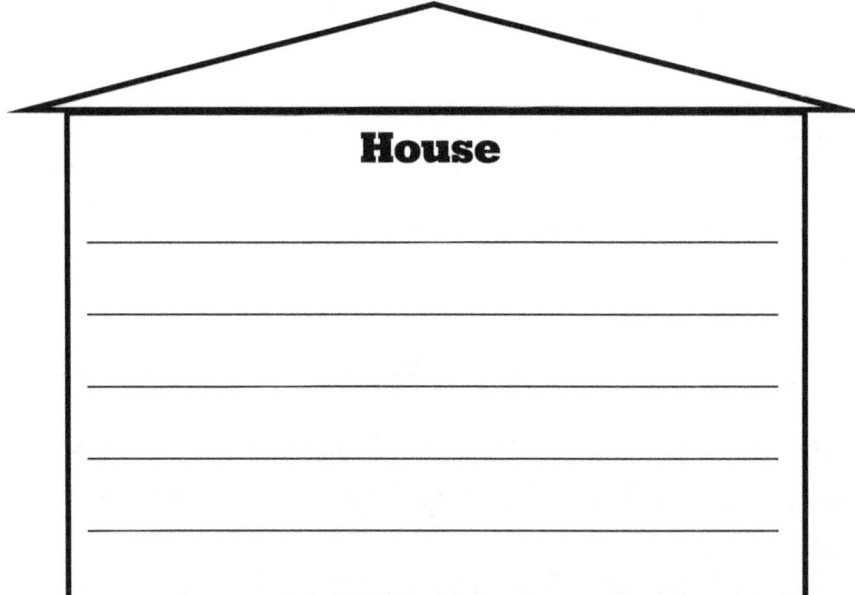

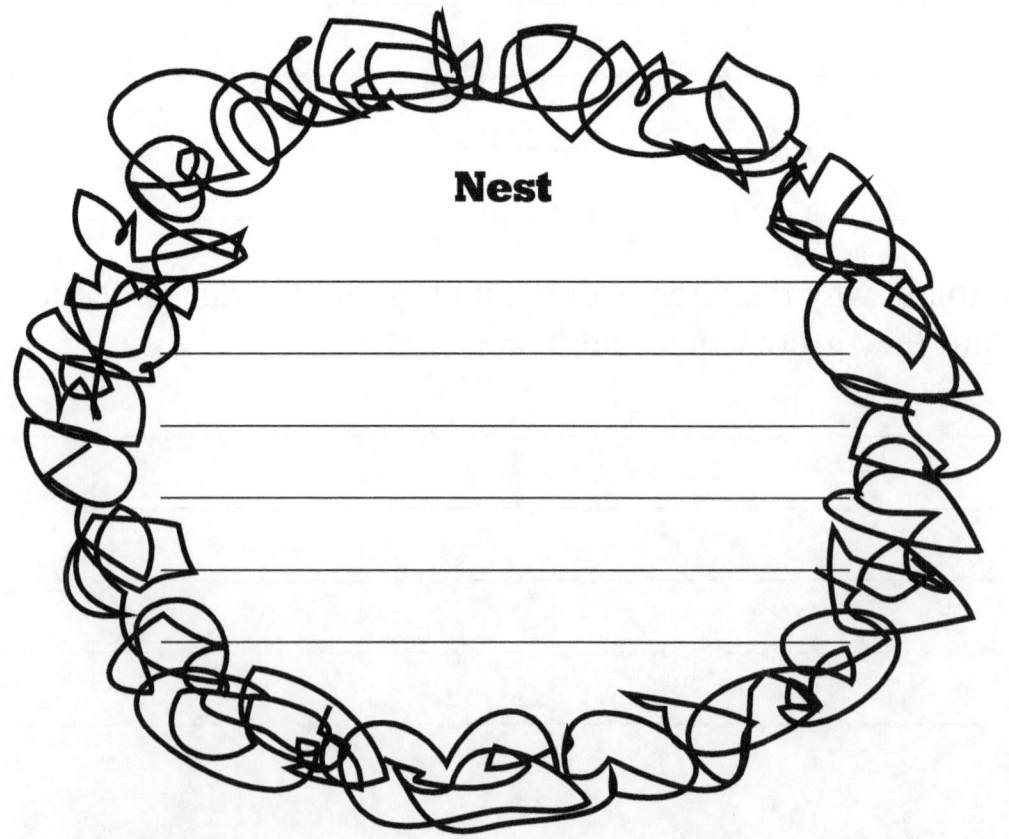

The Magic Finger **Sample Test**

Name_____ Date_____

In the book *The Magic Finger*, the Greggs learned an important lesson.

What lesson did they learn?

    and

How did they learn the lesson?

Give details and examples from the story to support your answer.

_____
_____
_____
_____
_____
_____
_____
_____
_____
_____
_____
_____
_____

Fantastic Mr. Fox

Key Vocabulary

farmer	valley	crooks
robber	beast	flask
shovels	tunnel	tractor
crater	tents	feast
loot	cement	

Vocabulary Instruction

Introduce the selected vocabulary words. Model the correct pronunciation, and elicit the meanings of each word. Allow the students to use the words orally in context. Play the game, "I'm Thinking Of A Word…." The students work in pairs. Each student is given a list of the selected vocabulary words. One student begins, "I'm thinking of a word…" and proceeds to say the definition or description of one of the vocabulary words. The other student guesses which word he or she is thinking of. The students take turns guessing and providing definitions and descriptions. Points may be awarded for each correctly guessed word.

Focus On Phonics

R-Blends: br, cr, tr, fr, pr, dr, gr

L-Blends: bl, cl, fl, gl, pl, sl

Sample Word List

R-Blends
brown	cry	drop
afraid	grass	pray
try	trap	crush

L-Blends
black	clock	fly
blue	clap	glue
play	slip	please

Language Skills

Plural Nouns: Adding "es" or "s"
See Language Skills Activity Sheet on page 35.

Fantastic Mr. Fox   **Knowledge 1**

Name_____ Date_____

The Search

Directions: Uh Oh! Mr. Fox escaped from the three farmers by the skin of his tail. Pretend you are one of the farmers. Make up a wanted poster. Make sure you describe all of his characteristics. Include a picture of Mr. Fox.

👉 Wanted! 👈

Name   **Mr. Fox**

Hair Color _____

Eye Color _____

Height _____

Weight _____

Wanted for _____

_____

Characteristics _____

_____

_____

_____

Fantastic Mr. Fox   Knowledge 2

Name_____ Date_____

Who's Who?

Directions: Write the names of the characters next to their descriptions.

     Mr. Fox   Rat   Bunce   Boggins   Bean

1. Drank cider, thin as a pencil _____

2. Ate doughnuts and goose liver, short, bad temper _____

3. Greedy, stayed in the cider cellar _____

4. Smart, brave, cared for his family _____

5. Ate chickens for breakfast, very fat _____

Draw a picture of your favorite character.

24   *Learning Through Literacy*

Fantastic Mr. Fox   **Comprehension 1**

Name_____ Date_____

How to Catch A Fox

Directions: Explain and illustrate three different ways the farmers tried to catch Mr. Fox.

One

Two

Three

Fantastic Mr. Fox 25

Fantastic Mr. Fox   **Comprehension 2**

Name_____ Date_____

What Next?

Directions: At the end of the story, the three farmers are still waiting for Mr. Fox to come out of his hole. What do you think that Mr. Fox and his family did next? Predict what the Foxes will do after they finish their great feast.

_____
_____
_____
_____
_____
_____
_____

Illustrate your prediction.

Fantastic Mr. Fox Application 1

Name _____ Date _____

The Plan

Directions: Pretend you are one of the three farmers. Make up your own plan for how you would catch the foxes. Write your answer on the lines below and then illustrate each answer.

First, I would	Then, I would

Next, I would	Finally, I would

Fantastic Mr. Fox Application 2

Name_____ Date_____

What is it?

Directions: Classify the characters as human, animal or thing on the lines next to their names.

| Mr. Fox | _____ |

| Bunce | _____ |

| Mabel | _____ |

| Badger | _____ |

| Bean | _____ |

| Carrot | _____ |

Fantastic Mr. Fox Analysis 1

Name_____ Date_____

Who is Mr. Fox?

Directions: Create a web of Mr. Fox's characteristics.

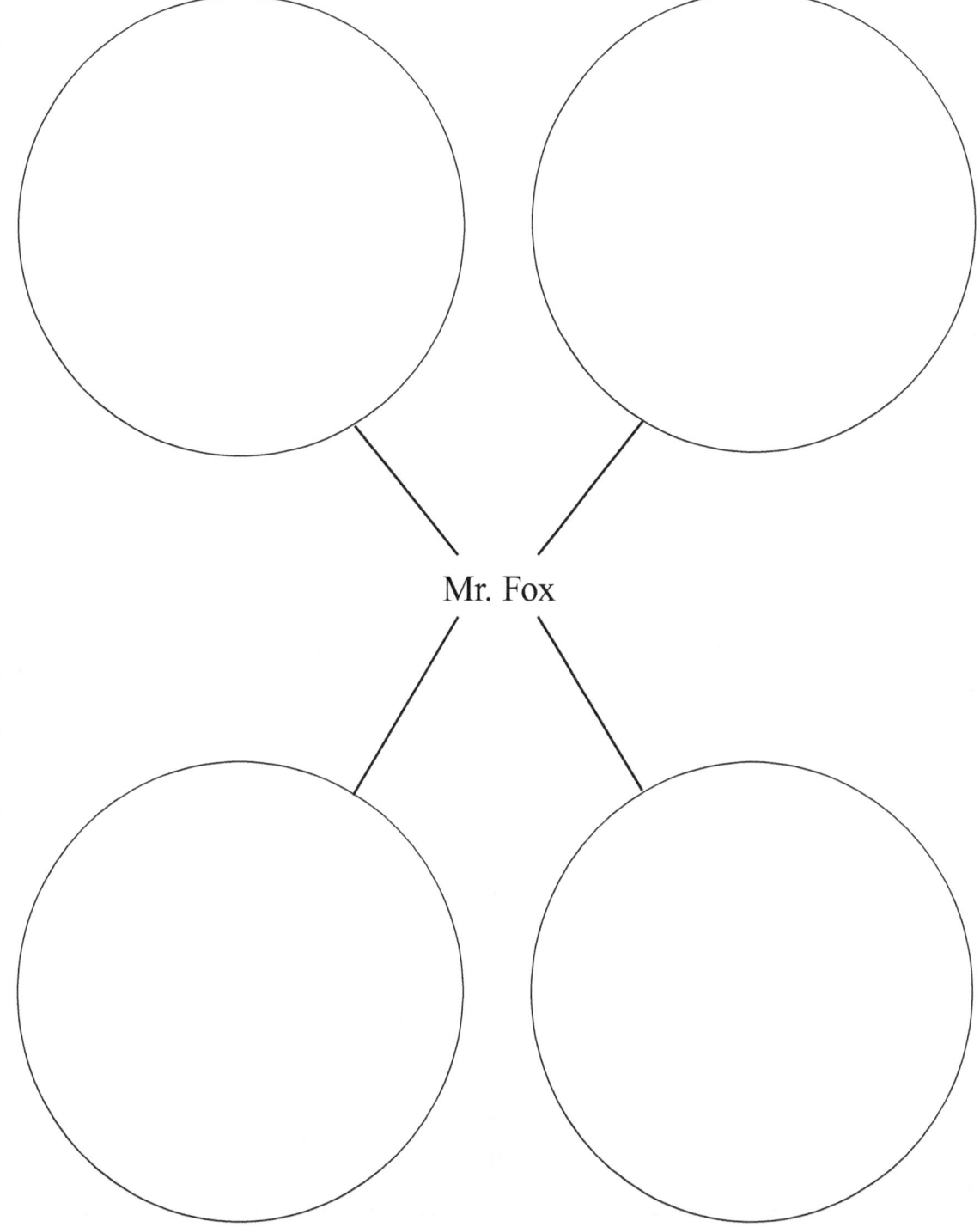

Fantastic Mr. Fox   Analysis 2

Name_____ Date_____

What's the Story?

Directions: Illustrate a story map for Fantastic Mr. Fox using the boxes below.

Beginning	**Problem**
Events	**Ending**

Fantastic Mr. Fox   Synthesis 1

Name_____   Date_____

Dear Diary

Directions: After Mr. Fox lost his tail, he became trapped in his hole with his family. Pretend you are Mr. Fox. Write in your diary about how you felt and what you thought about during the days you and your family were starving.

Day One

Date_____

Dear Diary,

_____
_____
_____
_____
_____

Day Two

Date_____

Dear Diary,

_____
_____
_____
_____
_____

Fantastic Mr. Fox Synthesis 2

Name_____ Date_____

Rhyme Time

Directions: The children would sing this song when they saw the farmers:

> Boggis and Bunce and Bean
> One fat, one short, one lean
> These horrible crooks
> So different in looks
> Were nonetheless equally mean

Create your own song or poem about Mr. Fox. Try to use words that rhyme.

_____
_____
_____
_____
_____

Illustrate your song or poem.

Fantastic Mr. Fox   **Evaluation 1**

Name_____ Date_____

Make Your Case

Directions: Badger worried that he and Mr. Fox were stealing. If you were Mr. Fox, how would you justify taking chickens, geese and cider from the farmers? Form at least two arguments below.

Argument #1

I am not really stealing because

_____
_____
_____
_____
_____
_____

Argument #2

I am not really stealing because

_____
_____
_____
_____
_____
_____

Fantastic Mr. Fox Evaluation 2

Name_____ Date_____

Is It True?

Directions: Judge whether parts of the story could have happened in real life. Justify your answers.

Could Happen in Real Life   Because

_____   _____

_____   _____

_____   _____

_____   _____

_____   _____

Could Not Happen in Real Life   Because

_____   _____

_____   _____

_____   _____

_____   _____

_____   _____

Fantastic Mr. Fox　　　　　　　　　　　　　　　　　　　　　　　　**Language Skills**

Name_____　Date_____

Plural Nouns

More Than One Fox?
Most nouns show their PLURAL (more than one) by adding *s*.
　　Example: more than one egg = eggs
If a noun ends in *sh*, *ch*, *x* or *ss*, we add *es* to show the plural.
　　Example: more than one fox = foxes

Directions: Carefully read the nouns below. Decide whether you need to add *s* or *es* to make the noun plural. Write the plural noun on the line next to each word.

1. fence _____　　9. guess _____

2. egg _____　　10. ax _____

3. chicken _____　　11. road _____

4. grass _____　　12. dish _____

5. floor _____　　13. fish _____

6. farmer _____　　14. house _____

7. box _____　　15. tent _____

8. dress _____

Fantastic Mr. Fox   **Sample Test**

Name_____ Date_____

Sample Test, Part 1

Directions: Read this selection from *Fantastic Mr. Fox*. Then answer questions 1–7.

For three days and three nights this waiting game went on.

"How long can a fox go without food or water?" Boggis asked on the third day.

"Not much longer now," Bean told him. "He'll make a run for it soon. He'll have to."

Bean was right. Down in the tunnel, the foxes were slowly but surely starving to death.

"If only we could have a small sip of water," said one of the small foxes. "Oh, Dad, can't you do something?"

"Couldn't we make a dash for it, Dad? We'd have a little bit of a chance, wouldn't we?"

"No chance at all," snapped Mrs. Fox. "I refuse to let you go up there and face those guns. I'd sooner you stay down here and die in peace."

Mr. Fox had not spoken for a long time. He had been sitting quite still, his eyes closed, not even hearing what the others were saying. Mrs. Fox knew that he was trying desperately to think of a way out. And now, as she looked at him, she saw him stir himself and get slowly to his feet. He looked back at his wife. There was a little spark of excitement dancing in his eyes.

"What is it, darling?" said Mrs. Fox quickly.

"I've just had a bit of an idea," Mr. Fox said carefully.

"What?" they cried. "Oh, Dad, what is it?"

"Come on!" said Mrs. Fox. "Tell us quickly!"

Fantastic Mr. Fox   **Sample Test**

Name_____ Date_____

"Well…" said Mr. Fox, then he stopped and sighed and sadly shook his head. He sat down again. "It's no good," he said. "It won't work after all."

"Why not, Dad?"

"Because it means more digging and we aren't any of us strong enough for that after three days and three nights without food."

"Yes we are, Dad!" cried the small foxes, jumping up and running to their father. "We can do it! You see if we can't! So can you!"

Mr. Fox looked at the four small foxes and he smiled. "What fine children I have," he thought. "They are starving to death and they haven't had a drink for three days, but they are still undefeated. I must not let them down."

"I suppose we could give it a try," he said.

"Let's go, Dad! Tell us what you want us to do!"

Slowly, Mrs. Fox got to her feet. She was suffering more than any of them from lack of food and water. She was very weak. "I am so sorry," she said, "but I don't think I'm going to be much help."

"You stay right where you are, my darling," said Mr. Fox. "We can handle this by ourselves."

Fantastic Mr. Fox   **Sample Test**

Name_____ Date_____

1. What is this selection mostly about?
   A. digging
   B. eating
   C. looking for food
   D. not giving up

2. The phrase "Make a run for it" means
   A. attack
   B. try to escape
   C. steal food
   D. run in a race

3. Why were the Foxes so weak?
   A. because they were sick
   B. because they lost their tails
   C. because they were starving
   D. because they were hopeless

4. Why hadn't Mr. Fox spoken for a long time?
   A. He was sleeping.
   B. He was eating.
   C. He was thinking of a plan.
   D. He was angry.

5. When Mr. Fox said he had an idea, the small foxes
   A. became excited to help their father.
   B. became very sick.
   C. began to fight with one another.
   D. began to complain.

6. Mrs. Fox did not go with her family because
   A. she was cooking.
   B. she was cleaning.
   C. she was too weak.
   D. she was too scared.

7. After reading the selection, which of the following statements about Mr. Fox seems to be true?
   A. He is a caring father and husband.
   B. He is a coward.
   C. He is lazy.
   D. He feels defeated by the farmers.

38 Learning Through Literacy

Fantastic Mr. Fox   **Sample Test**

Name_____ Date_____

Sample Test, Part 2

Directions: You are going to listen to a chapter from *Fantastic Mr. Fox* called "The Terrible Shovels." Then you will answer two questions about the chapter.

Listen to the chapter twice. The first time you hear the chapter, only listen carefully. The second time you hear the chapter, take notes on what you hear. Then use your notes to help you answer the questions.

NOTES
―――――――――――――――――――――――――――――――――

Fantastic Mr. Fox   **Sample Test**

Name_____ Date_____

1. Below is a web of different feelings the Foxes had during the chapter. Choose two feelings from the web. Explain why the Foxes felt this way. Be sure to use details from the chapter.

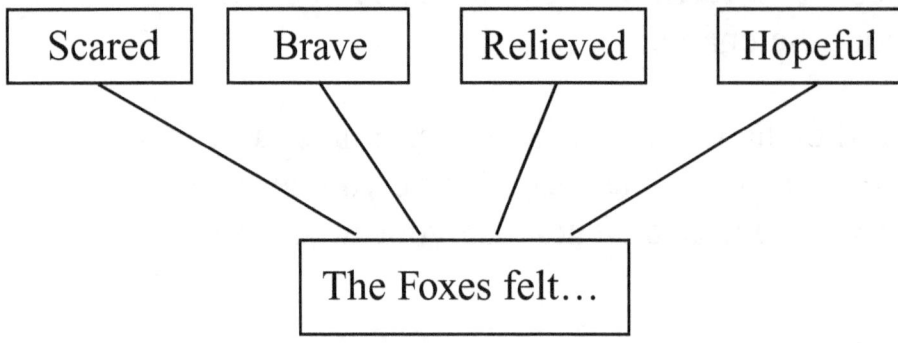

Feeling #1

_____
_____
_____

Feeling #2

_____
_____
_____

2. Explain why you think the chapter was titled "The Terrible Shovels."
   ■ Use details from the story to support your answer.
   Check your writing for correct spelling, capitalization and punctuation.

_____
_____
_____

40 Learning Through Literacy

Fantastic Mr. Fox   **Sample Test**

Name_____ Date_____

Sample Test: Part 3

Directions: You are going to read a chapter from *Fantastic Mr. Fox* called "The Feast." Then you will answer a question about what you have read. You can look back in the chapter to help you answer the question.

1. Because of the danger above ground, the animals decided they would have to live underground forever.
   - Explain why it was dangerous to go above ground.
   - Describe in your own words how the animals would live in "their underground village."
   - Explain why the animals were happy about living underground forever.

Check your writing for correct spelling and punctuation.

_____
_____
_____
_____
_____
_____
_____
_____
_____
_____
_____

The Twits

Key Vocabulary

twit   revolting   grand
horrid   ordinary   trousers
gradual   dangling   solemn
cylinder   parachute   knickers
wretched   crept   crouched
ridiculous mention   giddy

Vocabulary Instruction
Introduce selected vocabulary words. Model the correct pronunciation and define the words for the students. Write each vocabulary word on an index card. Write incomplete sentences on chart paper. Have the students select the correct word to complete each sentence. Students can read each sentence. Review the meanings of each word.

Focus On Phonics

R-Controlled Vowels: ar, ir, or, ur, er   **S Blends:** sn, sp, sw, sl, st, sk

Sample Word List

R-Controlled Vowels

car	or	burn
art	for	hurt
dart	corn	bird
her	shirt	third

S Blends

snap	swim	stick
snip	swam	storm
spot	slap	sky
swing	slip	skip

Language Skills
Punctuation: Using periods, question marks, and exclamation points correctly
See Language Skills Activity Sheet on page 55.

The Twits Knowledge 1

Name_____ Date_____

The Twits

Directions: Draw a picture of Mr. Twit and Mrs. Twit in the picture frames below.

Mr. Twit **Mrs. Twit**

The Twits Knowledge 2

Name_____ Date_____

Make A Match

Directions: Carefully read each sentence below. Match each sentence with the character who said it. Write the letter on the line next to the correct sentence.

_____ 1. "Hey! My spaghetti is moving!"

a. Roly-Poly Bird

b. one sticky little boy

_____ 2. "I always grow plenty of spiky thistles and plenty of stinging nettles. They keep out the nasty, nosy little children."

c. Mr. Twit

d. The Ravens

_____ 3. "We are only stuck by the seat of our pants!"

e. Muggle-Wump

_____ 4. "I've come for a holiday. I like to travel."

f. Mrs. Twit

_____ 5. "I'm not joking. We're going to turn both Mr. And Mrs. Twit upside down with their legs in the air!"

_____ 6. "They're coming back! They're coming back!"

The Twits **Comprehension 1**

Name_____ Date_____

Lots of Tricks!

Directions: Mr. and Mrs. Twit play lots of tricks on each other. Carefully read the sentences at the bottom of the page. Pick the trick you think was the funniest and cut out the sentence. Glue the sentence under the box. In the box, draw a picture that shows the trick.

Mrs. Twit put her glass eye in Mr. Twit's beer.	Mr. Twit put a frog in Mrs. Twit's bed.
Mrs. Twit fed Mr. Twit worms.	Mr. Twit tricked Mrs. Twit into thinking she was shrinking.

The Twits   **Comprehension 2**

Name_____ Date_____

Muggle-Wump

Directions: Muggle-Wump's feelings changed in different parts of the book. Carefully read each sentence below. Draw a picture of an event that made Muggle-Wump feel that way in the box next to each sentence.

1. Muggle-Wump felt miserable.

2. Muggle-Wump felt smart.

3. Muggle-Wump felt nervous.

4. Muggle-Wump felt happy.

The Twits Application 1

Name_____ Date_____

Hugtight Sticky Glue

Directions: Mr. Twit uses Hugtight Sticky Glue to catch birds in The Big Dead Tree. He almost caught four boys with it! Think of two other things Mr. Twit might catch with his Hugtight Sticky Glue. Write them on the lines below.

1. _____

2. _____

Directions: Mrs. Twit makes Bird Pie with the birds Mr. Twit catches. Using the things you wrote on the lines above, draw a new meal Mrs. Twit would have to make on each plate below. Write the name of the meal on the line under the plate.

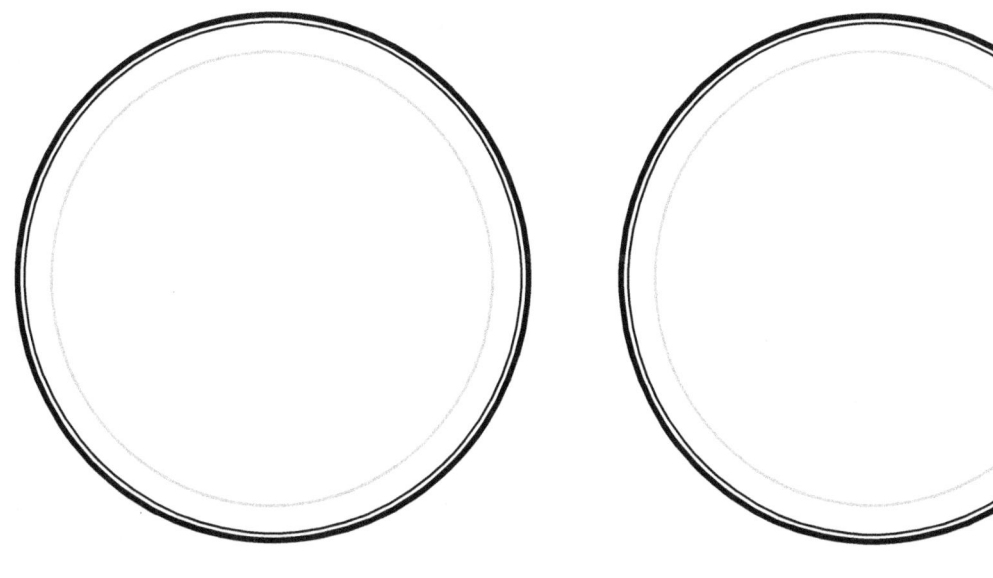

_____   _____

The Twits Application 2

Name_____ Date_____

Ballooning Away

Directions: Mr. Twit played another nasty trick on Mrs. Twit. He sent her ballooning up into the sky. Write what would happen to Mrs. Twit if she went ballooning away. Draw a picture in the box to illustrate your answer.

The Twits Analysis 1

Name_____ Date_____

Who's Who?

Directions: Think about the characters in the story. Under the character's name, write five words to describe them.

Mr. Twit

_____
_____
_____
_____
_____

Mrs. Twit

_____
_____
_____
_____
_____

Muggle-Wump

_____
_____
_____
_____
_____

Roly-Poly Bird

_____
_____
_____
_____
_____

What's The Difference?

The Twits   **Analysis 2**

Name_____ Date_____

Directions: Use the Venn diagram below to compare and contrast Muggle-Wump and Roly-Poly Bird.

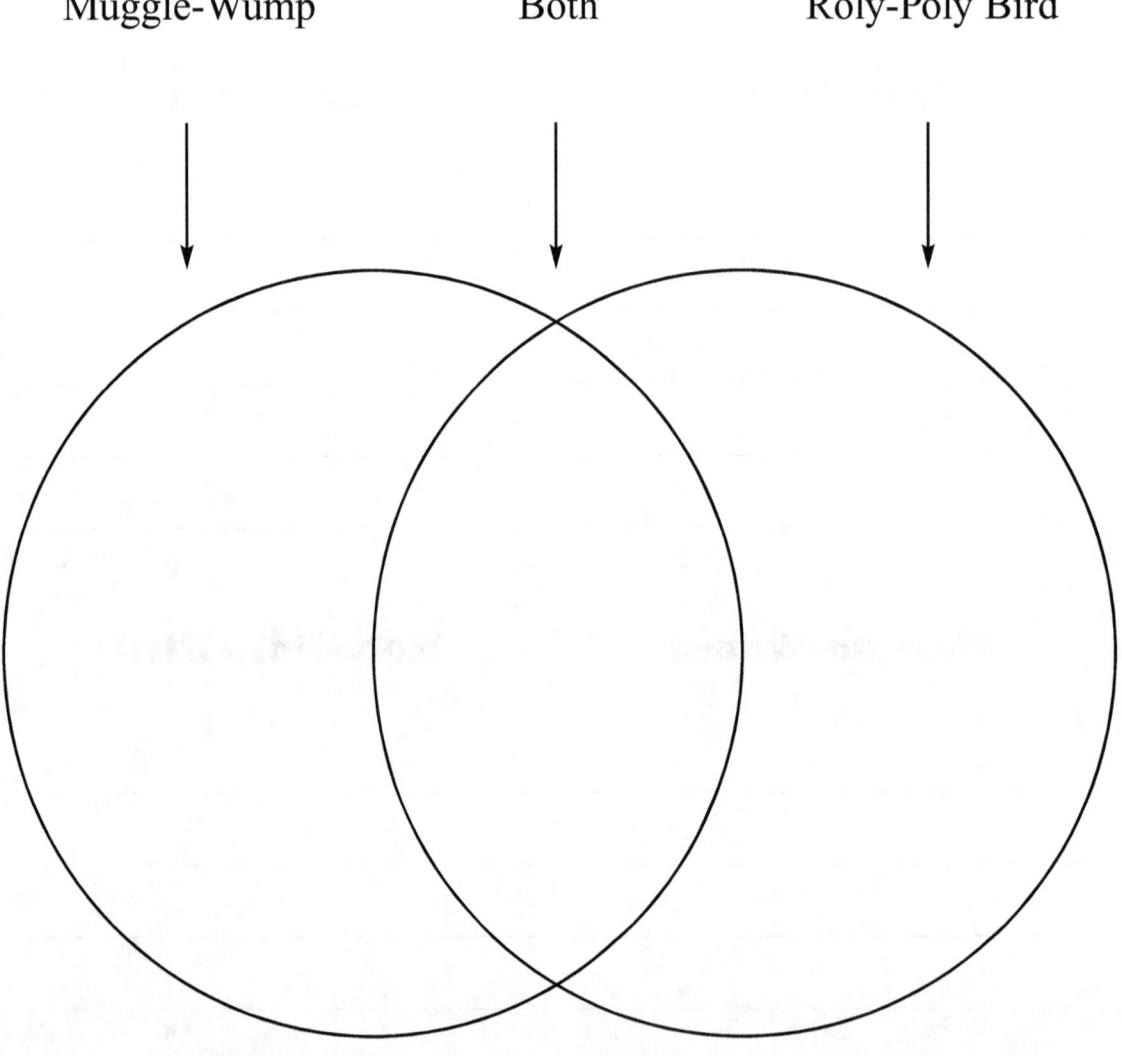

50 *Learning Through Literacy*

The Twits   **Synthesis 1**

Name_____ Date_____

You Name It!

Directions: Create a new title for the story. Use at least three examples from the story to explain why you chose your title.

_____

New Title

_____
_____
_____
_____
_____
_____
_____
_____
_____
_____
_____

The Twits Synthesis 2

Name_____ Date_____

An Idea!

Muggle-Wump had a great idea. He had all the animals turn the Twits' furniture upside down so they would stand on their heads for hours.

Directions: Think about all the bad things the Twits did to the Muggle-Wump family. On the lines below, write another way the Muggle-Wump family could get even with the Twits.

_____
_____
_____
_____
_____
_____
_____
_____
_____
_____
_____
_____
_____

The Twits — Evaluation 1

Name_____ Date_____

Read It!

Directions: Write a letter to a friend. Tell your friend whether or not he or she should read *The Twits*.

In your letter
- Tell three things you liked about the story
    OR
- Tell three things you didn't like about the story

Dear _____ ,

_____
_____
_____
_____
_____
_____
_____
_____
_____
_____
_____

Your friend,

_____

The Twits　　　　　　　　　　　　　　　　　　　　　　　　　　　　**Evaluation 2**

Name_____ Date_____

You Be the Judge

Directions: Carefully read each sentence below. Decide if each sentence is true or false. Write *true* or *false* on the line next to each sentence.

_____ Mrs. Twit was a beautiful woman.

_____ The Muggle-Wump family was happy living in the cage.

_____ The Roly-Poly Bird came from Africa.

_____ Mr. Twit hated Muggle-Wump and his family.

_____ The Muggle-Wump family painted Hugtight Sticky Glue all over the ceiling.

_____ The animals wanted the Twits to think they were upside down.

_____ The Roly-Poly Bird was very helpful.

_____ Two black ravens dropped glue on the Twits' heads.

_____ Muggle-Wump and his family were sad to leave the Twits.

_____ The Twits got the shrinks and disappeared.

The Twits **Language Skills**

Name_____ Date_____

Perfect Punctuation

A PERIOD (.) goes at the end of a sentence that tells something.
   Example: That boy is nice.

A QUESTION MARK (?) goes at the end of a sentence that asks something.
   Example: Do you like ice cream?

An EXCLAMATION MARK (!) goes at the end of a sentence that tells something important.
   Example: The car is on fire!

Directions: Carefully read each sentence. Decide whether each sentence should have a period, question mark or exclamation mark at the end. Write the correct punctuation.

1. Mr. Twit had a beard

2. What is in my spaghetti

3. You've got the shrinks

4. Mrs. Twit is going to cook the boys with carrots

5. Four monkeys lived in the cage

6. Where did the Roly-Poly Bird come from

7. Quick, get the key

8. How can we turn the Twits upside down

9. The carpet was enormous

10. How will Muggle-Wump and his family escape

Test-Taking Skills 2

Skimming

Aim: How do we skim a passage?

Objectives
1. Students will understand the difference between skimming and scanning.
2. Students will search reading passages for important details.
3. Students will adjust their purposes and rates of reading.

Procedures
These activities are designed to be part of ongoing instruction, not one isolated lesson.

- Introduce the term *skim* and teach the meaning of the word.

  Skimming is reading fast. It gives you the main idea of a story or paragraph. Use it when you need to know what the paragraph is mostly about.

- Elicit from students different situations when they would skim.

- Teach the students the following strategies for skimming:
  - Decide what information you need to know.
  - Look for key words.
  - Locate the information and select the appropriate answer.

- Give the students worksheets or activities where they can practice skimming for the main idea.

- Give students opportunities during content area lessons to skim passages in order to find the topic.

- Bring in advertisements from magazines and newspapers. Let the students skim the page and decide what is being sold.

- Give one question assignments about a reading passage. Let the students skim the passage to find the appropriate information.

- Assess mastery of the skill. Reteach and review as necessary.

The Twits

Name_____ Date_____

Sample Test, Part One

Directions: Read this selection from *The Twits*. Then answer questions 1–6.

Mrs. Twit was no better than her husband. She did not, of course, have a hairy face. It was a pity she didn't because that, at any rate, would have hidden some of her fearful ugliness.

But the funny thing is Mrs. Twit wasn't born ugly. She'd had quite a nice face when she was young. The ugliness had grown upon her year by year as she got older.

Why would that happen? I'll tell you why.

If a person has ugly thoughts, it begins to show on their face. And when that person has ugly thoughts every day, every week, every year, the face gets so ugly you can hardly bear to look at it.

A person who has good thoughts cannot ever be ugly. You can have a wonky nose and a crooked mouth and a double chin and stick-out teeth, but if you have good thoughts they will shine out of your face like sunbeams and you will always look lovely.

Nothing good shone out of Mrs. Twit's face.

In her right hand she carried a walking stick. She used to tell people that this was because she had warts growing on the sole of her left foot and walking was painful. But the real reason she carried a stick was so she could hit things with it, things like dogs and small children.

The Twits   **Sample Test**

Name _____ Date _____

1. What is the selection mostly about?
   A. ugly people
   B. old people
   C. Mrs. Twit
   D. young girls

2. What are "ugly thoughts"?
   A. mean thoughts
   B. nasty thoughts
   C. unkind thoughts
   D. all of the above

3. Mrs. Twit became ugly because
   A. she got old.
   B. she was born ugly.
   C. she has ugly thoughts.
   D. she had a wonky nose.

4. A person who has good thoughts can never be ugly because
   A. good thoughts shine out of their face.
   B. they are quiet.
   C. they have stick-out teeth.
   D. they have a double chin.

5. Which word best describes Mrs. Twit?
   A. nice
   B. happy
   C. ugly
   D. small

6. The real reason Mrs. Twit had a walking stick was
   A. so she could look prettier.
   B. so she could hit children and small animals.
   C. to help her walk.
   D. because she was old.

The Twits — Sample Test

Name_____ Date_____

Sample Test, Part 2

Directions: You are going to listen to a chapter from *The Twits* called "Hugtight Sticky Glue." Then you will answer two questions about the chapter.

Listen to the chapter twice. The first time you hear the chapter, only listen carefully. The second time you hear the chapter, take notes on what you hear. Then use your notes to help you answer the questions.

NOTES

The Twits   **Sample Test**

Name_____ Date_____

1. Explain how Mr. Twit caught the birds for Wednesday's Bird Pie Supper. Use sequence words to help make your answer clear.

_____
_____
_____
_____
_____
_____
_____

2. The name of this chapter is "Hugtight Sticky Glue." Create a new name for the chapter. Use details from the chapter to explain why you chose this name.

_____
New Title

_____
_____
_____
_____
_____
_____
_____

The Twits   Sample Test

Name_____   Date_____

Sample Test, Part 3

Directions: You are going to read a chapter from *The Twits* called "The Great Upside Down Circus" and another chapter called "The Roly-Poly Bird to the Rescue." Then you will answer questions about both chapters. You can look back in the chapters to help you answer the questions.

1. Read these sentences from the chapter:

    Muggle-Wump and his family longed to escape from the cage in Mr. Twit's garden and go back to the African jungle where they came from. They hated Mr. and Mrs. Twit for making their lives miserable.

    Explain how Mr. and Mrs. Twit made the monkeys' lives miserable. Use details from the chapter in your answer.

    _____
    _____
    _____
    _____
    _____

2. Write three ways that Muggle-Wump and Roly-Poly Bird are the same. Use details from the chapter in your answer.

    1. _____
    2. _____
    3. _____

George's Marvelous Medicine

Key Vocabulary

mischief	saucer	tremendous	pondering
medicine	enormous	shrill	forbidden
splendid	marvelous	wizardry	brim
jug	tiresome	suspended	puncture
rubbish	bullocks	crane	notice
frisky	supply	hesitate	cockerel
anxiously	snatched		

Vocabulary Instruction

Introduce selected vocabulary words, and discuss their definitions. Model using the words orally in context. Ask student volunteers to provide sentences using the words. On chart paper or chalkboard, write the definition of a vocabulary word. Have the students play hangman to match the definition to the word.

Focus On Phonics

Silent e Rule: When we add a silent e, the vowel says its own name.
Vowel Teams Rule: When vowels are teamed together, the first vowel says its own name.

Sample Word List

Silent e
came   bike   these
game   hike   use
bone   line   stone

Vowel Teams
boat   day
rail   goal   say
eat   keep   sea

Language Skills

Suffixes: Adding suffixes to a root word to change the words meaning
See Language Skills Activity Sheet on page 75.

62   Learning Through Literacy

George's Marvelous Medicine Knowledge 1

Name _____ Date _____

George's Patients

Directions: Make a list of the people and animals that took a dose of George's Marvelous Medicine One.

_____

_____

_____

_____

_____

Illustrate what happened to one of the characters or animals after taking a dose of George's Marvelous Medicine One.

George's Marvelous Medicine   Knowledge 2

Name_____ Date_____

Mixed-Up Medicine

Directions: Match the different effects of George's Medicine. Choose a sentence from the box below and write it on the line next to the correct medicine.

| It made only their legs taller. | It made them smaller. |
| It made only their necks longer. | It made their bodies bigger. |

George's Marvelous Medicine One
_____

George's Marvelous Medicine Two
_____

George's Marvelous Medicine Three
_____

George's Marvelous Medicine Four
_____
_____

Illustrate what happened to Grandma after she drank George's Marvelous Medicine One.

64 *Learning Through Literacy*

George's Marvelous Medicine   Comprehension 1

Name_____ Date_____

Who Said That?

Directions: Carefully read each statement below. On the line next to each statement, write the name of the characters in *George's Marvelous Medicine* who said it. The names of the characters are listed in the box at the top of the page. You may choose each character more than once.

| George   Grandma   Mr. Kranky   Mrs. Kranky |

1. "You know what's the matter with _____
   you? You're growing too fast.
   Boys who grow too fast become
   stupid and lazy."

2. "I'm not going to be frightened _____
   by her."

3. "Is it time for my medicine yet?" _____

4. "George, how much of this _____
   medicine have you got?"

5. "I'm not leaving my own mother _____
   sticking up through the roof for
   the rest of her life."

6. "We will build a Marvelous _____
   Medicine Factory and sell the
   stuff in bottles at ten dollars apiece."

7. "I can't possibly remember all the _____
   hundreds of things I put in the pot
   to make medicine."

George's Marvelous Medicine	Comprehension 2

Name_____ Date_____

Bad Reaction

Directions: Immediately after Grandma had taken a dose of George's Marvelous Medicine One, strange things began to happen to her body. Write five sentences that retell Grandma's reaction to the medicine.

_____
_____
_____
_____
_____

Illustrate what Grandma looked like after she had a dose of George's medicine.

George's Marvelous Medicine   Application 1

Name _____ Date _____

Grandma's Dinner

Directions: In the beginning of the story, Grandma told George to eat caterpillars, worms, slugs and other creatures. She especially loved beetles. Create a meal for grandma. Be sure to use her favorite ingredients.

Ingredients:

_____

_____

_____

_____

Illustrate what Grandma's meal looks like on the plate below.

George's Marvelous Medicine   Application 2

Name_____ Date_____

City Limits

Directions: Uh oh! After Grandma drank the medicine she grew so tall she went through the roof of the house. Imagine if she lived in the city. Compare the city to a farm.

City	Farm
_____	_____
_____	_____
_____	_____
_____	_____
_____	_____

How might her size affect daily city life? Explain how people in the city would react to the GIANT GRANDMA.

_____
_____
_____
_____

George's Marvelous Medicine   Analysis 1

Name_____ Date_____

Real vs. Pretend

Directions: Write the word REAL next to the sentence that could happen in real life. Write the word PRETEND next to the sentence that could not happen in real life.

_____ A grandmother can be a mean woman.

_____ A boy can live with his grandma.

_____ A person can grow to be the size of a two-story house.

_____ A person can eat bugs.

_____ Medicine can make a chicken grow bigger than a person.

_____ A person can drink brown paint and feel better.

Choose from the sentences above. Write one in the REAL box and one in the PRETEND box. Illustrate the sentences in the boxes.

REAL	**PRETEND**

George's Marvelous Medicine   Analysis 2

Name _____ Date _____

What's the Problem?

Directions: Complete the story map below. Think about what George's main problem was and what he did to try to solve it.

BEGINNING	PROBLEM

EVENTS	ENDING

George's Marvelous Medicine   Synthesis 1

Name_____ Date_____

All Bottled Up

Directions: Wow! George made some marvelous medicine. Pretend you are going to sell it. Design a label for George's medicine bottle. Be sure to tell what it is used for and list all the ingredients.

George's Marvelous Medicine   **Synthesis 2**

Name_____   Date_____

Wonderful Grandma!

Directions: Imagine that George's Marvelous Medicine One made Grandma into a beautiful and kind person instead of a gigantic and wicked witch. Explain how you think George would react to his new Grandma. How do you think this would change the book?

_____
_____
_____
_____

Illustrate how you think the new and wonderful Grandma would look.

George's Marvelous Medicine Evaluation 1

Name_____ Date_____

Read All About It!

Directions: Extra! Extra! George makes a marvelous medicine. Design a newspaper article about George's new medicine. Be sure to include in your article how it was made, what it does, and how it can be dangerous. Include a photograph of George on the front page.

The Farmtown Times

Date

Boy Makes New Marvelous Medicine

George's Marvelous Medicine Evaluation 2

Name_____ Date_____

Meet George!

Directions: Pretend you have been asked to do an interview with George for a magazine. Think of four questions you would ask him. Write how you think George would answer the questions on the lines below.

My Interview With George

Question: _____

George's Answer: _____

_____

Question: _____

George's Answer: _____

_____

Question: _____

George's Answer: _____

_____

Question: _____

George's Answer: _____

_____

Do you like George? Why or why not? _____

George's Marvelous Medicine Language Skills

Name_____ _____ Date

Adding Suffixes

A **suffix** is a group of letters that when added to the end of a word, change the word's meaning. Here are some suffixes and their meanings.

Suffix	Meaning
er	more
est	most
ful	full of
less	without

Directions: Add the suffix to each word below. Write the new word on the first line. Write the meaning of each new word on the second line.

	New Word	Meaning
Fast + er =	_____	_____
Fast + est =	_____	_____
dark + er =	_____	_____
dark + est =	_____	_____
thank+ ful =	_____	_____
wish = ful =	_____	_____
end + less =	_____	_____
help+ less =	_____	_____

Test-Taking Skills 3

Use Time Wisely

Aim: How do we use time when taking a test?

Objectives
1. The students will recognize that they have a limited amount of time to complete a test.
2. The students will spend an appropriate amount of time on a test question and then move on.
3. The students will remain relaxed when taking a test with time limits.

Procedures
Most students in special education have extended time available. However, it is still beneficial that they learn to move from one question to another. Sticking with any task too long can lead to frustration.

Use countdowns to encourage students to get things done in a limited time period. For example, say, "On the count of 10, have your math books open to page 16."

- Teach the students the following time management strategies
  - Listen carefully to directions.
  - Repeat the directions to yourself.
  - Ask questions before a test begins.
  - Look ahead to see how much you have to complete.
  - First answer the questions you know, then go back to the ones you skipped.
  - Use all your time. If you finish early, go back and check your work.

- Write the beginning and expected end time of any classroom test on the board. Allow the students to compute how many minutes they have to complete the test.

- When giving any test or assessment, elicit from the students how much time seems appropriate to spend on each question.

- Assess the students' time management skills. Keep reinforcing and reteaching.

Note: *When teaching time management (or any other test-taking skill), it is very important to remind the students that IT IS ONLY A TEST! If they do not finish the whole test, the world will keep turning, their parents will still love them and the tide will still come in. Just let them know their best effort is what counts.*

George's Marvelous Medicine   Sample Test

Name_____   Date_____

Sample Test, Part 1

Directions: Read the chapter "The Marvelous Plan" from *George's Marvelous Medicine*. Then answer questions 1–6.

George sat himself down at the table in the kitchen. He was shaking a little. Oh, how he hated Grandma! He really hated that horrid old witchy woman. And all of a sudden he had a tremendous urge to do something about her. Something whopping. Something absolutely terrific. A real shocker. A sort of explosion. He wanted to blow away the old witchy smell that hung about her in the next room. He may have been only eight years old, but he was a brave little boy. He was ready to take this old woman on.

"I'm not going to be frightened by her," he said softly to himself. But he was frightened. And that's why he wanted suddenly to explode her away.

Well… not quite away. But he did want to shake the old woman up a bit.

Very well, then, what should it be, this whopping terrific exploding shocker for Grandma?

He would have liked to put a firecracker under her chair, but he didn't have one.

He would have liked to put six big black rats in the room with her and lock the door, but he didn't have six big black rats.

As George sat there pondering this interesting problem, his eyes fell upon the bottle of Grandma's brown medicine standing on the sideboard. Rotten stuff it seemed to be. Four times a day, a large spoonful of it was shoveled into her mouth, and it didn't do her the slightest bit of good. She was always just as horrid after she'd had it as she'd been before. The whole point of medicine was to make a person better. If it didn't do that, then it was quite useless.

So-ho, thought George suddenly, Ah-ha! I know exactly what I'll do. I shall make her a new medicine, one that is so strong and so fierce and so fantastic it will either cure her completely or blow

George's Marvelous Medicine   **Sample Test**

off the top of her head. I'll make her a magic medicine, a medicine no doctor in the world has ever made before.

George looked at the kitchen clock. It said five past ten. There was nearly an hour left before Grandma's next dose was due at eleven.

"Here we go then!" cried George, jumping up from the table, "A magic medicine it shall be!"

---

1. What is this selection mostly about?
   A. a boy who gets into trouble
   B. a trip to the doctor
   C. a boy who decides on a plan
   D. a woman who is mean to her grandson

2. George was thinking about his grandmother because
   A. he wanted to get her a gift.
   B. He was frightened by her.
   C. She made him sad.
   D. She had a pet snake.

3. Which of the following was not one of the plans George thought about:
   A. putting a firecracker under her chair
   B. putting bugs in her soup
   C. putting a long green snake down her dress
   D. putting rats in her room

4. While George was thinking of a plan, his "eye fell upon"
   A. Grandma's medicine
   B. a beetle in the corner
   C. a green snake
   D. the clock

5. Why did George think that Grandma's medicine was useless?
   A. because she was still sick
   B. because she still had a fever
   C. because she was just as horrid as before she took the medicine
   D. because it didn't have the correct ingredients

6. What was George's final plan?
   A. to bring Grandma to the doctor
   B. to tell his parents about her behavior
   C. to put a long green snake down her dress
   D. to make her a new medicine

George's Marvelous Medicine   **Sample Test**

Name_____ Date_____

Sample Test, Part 2

Directions: You are going to listen to a selection from *George's Marvelous Medicine*. You will answer two questions about the selection.

Listen to the chapter twice. The first time you hear the chapter, only listen carefully. The second time you hear this selection, take notes on what you hear. Then use your notes to help you answer the questions.

NOTES

George's Marvelous Medicine **Sample Test**

Name_____ Date_____

1. Write how each of the following characters felt about George's medicine in the Feeling box beside his or her name and explain why you think they felt that way.

CHARACTER	FEELING
Mr. Kranky	
Mrs. Kranky	
George	

2. Explain why Mr. Kranky said, "We must start making more (medicine) at once! More and more and more!"

_____

_____

George's Marvelous Medicine — **Sample Test**

Name_____ Date_____

Sample Test, Part 3

Directions: Read the chapter "Goodbye, Grandma" from the book *George's Marvelous Medicine*. Answer the question below.

George felt that he had "touched with the very tips of his fingers the edge of a magic world."

Explain what George meant by this quote.

   and

Why did he feel this way?

_____
_____
_____
_____
_____
_____
_____
_____
_____
_____
_____
_____

The Witches

Key Vocabulary

ordinary	ravine	vanish	recognize	conceal
pheasant	lecture	coast	journey	compromise
acrobat	prevention	cruelty	motionless	adoration
mesmerized	transformed	boasting	bewildered	shrinking
ancient	climb	corridor	balcony	burglar
stench	tidy	scowl	mishap	appetite
wielding	envy	gadgets	omelets	imitating

Vocabulary Instruction
Introduce selected vocabulary words. Model correct pronunciation and discuss definition. Ask student volunteers to read each word and provide the definition. Review. Write each word on a card and each definition on a separate card. Students can review the vocabulary words by playing a memory game with the cards.

Focus On Phonics

Hard and Soft C Sounds　　　　**Hard and Soft G Sounds**

Sample Word List

Hard and Soft C		Hard and Soft G	
cat	mice	goat	change
coat	nice	get	magic
crush	fancy	gobble	gentle
cod	excite	wig	rage

Language Skills

Contractions: Forming and identifying contractions
See Language Skills Activity Sheet on page 95.

The Witches Knowledge 1

Name _____ Date _____

A REAL Witch

Directions: Grandmama told the boy how to recognize a witch. Draw a picture in the box below showing what a REAL WITCH looks like.

The Witches Knowledge 2

Name_____ Date_____

The Grand High Witch Of All the World

Directions: Use the question words below to help you describe the Grand High Witch of All the World.

Who is she?

_____

_____

What does she look like?

_____

_____

When does she meet the other witches?

_____

_____

Where does she hold her meetings?

_____

_____

Why does she hold these meetings?

_____

_____

The Witches   **Comprehension 1**

Name_____ Date_____

The Meeting

Directions: The boy in the story found himself in a dangerous place. He was stuck hiding behind a screen at the Witches Annual Convention! On the lines below, explain how the boy figured out that the women in the meeting were real witches.

Think about these clues: What were they wearing?
                                     What were they doing?
                                     What did the boy see happening?

_____

_____

_____

_____

_____

The Witches Comprehension 2

Name_____ Date_____

The Witches' Wicked Plan

Directions:
"Children are rree-volting!" screamed the Grand High Witch. "Vee vill vipe them all avay!" In your own words, outline the Grand High Witch's plan to destroy all the children of England. On the lines below, write the steps of her evil plan in the correct order.

First,_____

_____

_____

Next,_____

_____

_____

Then,_____

_____

_____

After that,_____

_____

_____

Soon,_____

_____

_____

Finally,_____

_____

The Witches Application 1

Name _____ Date _____

Formula 86 Delayed Action Mouse Maker

Directions: What is the recipe for the Formula 86 Delayed Action Mouse Maker? From the items listed below, select the correct ingredients. Circle the items that go in the recipe.

the wrong end of a telescope   apples
the tongue of a catspringer   fried mice tails
black ink   forty-five brown mice
frog-juice   bad milk
an alarm clock   the beak of a blabber snitch
a gruntle's egg   one school book
the snout of a grobblesquirt   cat's claws
a small girl's dress   the claw of a crabcruncher
nine red raindrops

Directions: The Grand High Witch warned the other witches, "Never put more than vun drop into each ssveet or chocolate." Why did she give this warning? On the lines below, write what would happen if a child ate more than one drop of the Formula 86 Delayed Action Mouse Maker.

_____
_____
_____
_____

The Witches Application 2

Name_____ Date_____

Trapped!

The witches smelled the boy and found him behind the screen. The next thing the boy knew, the witches had turned him into a mouse!

If you were in the boy's place, would you have been able to escape?

_____

Directions:
1. Tell your partner what you would have done if you were trapped.

2. Listen to what your partner says he or she would have done.

3. On the lines below, explain what you would have done if you were trapped behind the screen at the Witches' Annual Convention.

_____
_____
_____
_____
_____
_____
_____
_____
_____

The Witches Analysis 1

Name _____ Date _____

What's It All About?

Directions: Complete the story map below to tell about *The Witches*.

Characters:
_____
_____
_____

Settings:
_____
_____
_____

Title
_____
_____

Problem:
_____
_____
_____
_____
_____

Solution:
_____
_____
_____
_____
_____

The Witches Analysis 2

Name_____ Date_____

Same and Different

Directions: In each box below, draw a picture of Grandmama and a picture of the Grand High Witch.

Grandmama   The Grand High Witch

Directions: Look at the pictures you drew. Think about both characters. In the columns, write three ways they are the same and three ways they are different.

Things that are the same   Things that are different

1. _____   1. _____

   _____   _____

2. _____   2. _____

   _____   _____

3. _____   3. _____

   _____   _____

The Witches Synthesis 1

Name_____ Date_____

The Mouse Burglar

Eureka! They did it! Grandmama and the Boy (or should we say mouse) have stolen a bottle of Formula 86 Delayed Action Mouse Maker. What will happen next?

Directions: Under the name of each character, write what you predict will happen to that character.

The Boy

_____
_____
_____
_____

Grandmama

_____
_____
_____
_____

The Grand High Witch

_____
_____
_____
_____

Bruno

_____
_____
_____
_____

The Witches Synthesis 2

Name_____ Date_____

Read All About It!

Directions: In the space provided below, create a poster advertising *The Witches*. Draw you favorite scene from the book so that other people will want to read it.

THE WITCHES

Written by Roald Dahl

The Witches Evaluation 1

Name_____ Date_____

The Heart of A Mouse

Directions:
Which character from *The Witches* would you most like to meet? Grandmama? Bruno? The Boy (Mouse)? The Grand High Witch? Or would it be another character? On the lines below, write which character you would most like to meet.

Remember to tell:
- Who the character is.
- Why you would like to meet him or her.
- Where you would go with the character.
- What you would say to the character.

_____
_____
_____
_____
_____
_____
_____
_____
_____
_____
_____

The Witches   Evaluation 2

Name_____ Date_____

All the Best Parts

Directions: Answer the following questions about *The Witches*.

What was the funniest part of the book?

_____
_____
_____
_____

What was the scariest part of the book?

_____
_____
_____
_____

What was the saddest part of the book?

_____
_____
_____
_____

The Witches   **Language Skills**

Name_____ Date_____

Contraction Action

Contractions are made when two words are combined, one or more letters from the second word are left out and an apostrophe (') is put in place of the missing letters.

Examples: Was not= wasn't   you are=you're
                   he is = he's   she will= she'll

Directions: Fill in the worksheet to form your own contractions.

Two words	Cross out the letter(s) and add an apostrophe	Contraction
is not	is n~~o~~t	isn't
did not		
I will		
you are		
they are		
he is		
she is		

Test-Taking Skills 4

Using An Answer Sheet

Aim: How do we fill in an answer sheet?

Objectives
1. The students will recognize the purpose of an answer sheet.
2. The students will correctly fill in an answer sheet circle.
3. The students will be able to transfer their answers onto the answer sheet correctly.

Procedures
This is an extremely difficult skill for some students in special education. Some students' IEPs may dictate that someone transfer answers for them. For the remaining students, the following activities may assist their mastery of this skill.

- Have students practice filling in answer key circles correctly. Teach them that they must:
  - Color in the circle completely.
  - Choose only one circle in each row.
  - Erase any mistakes thoroughly.

- Provide the students with enlarged answer keys for the cumulative tests included in this book and any other teacher-made test.

- Teach the students how to go back and check the question number on the test with the question number on the answer key.

The Witches   **Sample Test**

Name_____ Date_____

Sample Test, Part 1

Directions: Read this selection from *The Witches*. Then answer questions 1–5.

In fairy tales, witches always wear silly black hats and black cloaks, and they ride on broomsticks.

But this is not a fairy tale. This is about REAL WITCHES.

The most important thing you should know about REAL WITCHES is this. Listen very carefully. Never forget what is coming next.

REAL WITCHES dress in ordinary clothes and look very much like ordinary women. They live in ordinary houses, and they work in ORDINARY JOBS.

That is why they are so hard to catch.

A REAL WITCH hates children with a red-hot sizzling hatred that is more sizzling and red-hot than any hatred you could possibly imagine.

A REAL WITCH spends all her time plotting to get rid of the children in her particular territory. Her passion is to do away with them, one by one. Even if she is working as a cashier in a supermarket or typing letters for a businessman or driving round in a fancy car (and she could be doing any of these things), it is all she thinks about the whole day long. Her mind will always be plotting and scheming and churning and burning and whizzing and phizzing with murderous bloodthirsty thoughts.

A REAL WITCH gets the same pleasure from squelching a child as you get from eating a plateful of strawberries and thick cream. Squish them and squiggle them and make them disappear. That is the motto of all witches.

The Witches   **Sample Test**

Name_____   Date_____

1. What is the selection mostly about?
   A. strawberries and cream
   B. real witches
   C. supermarket cashiers
   D. mean people

2. What does a witch wear?
   A. a black hat
   B. a black cloak
   C. a green hat
   D. normal women's clothes

3. What does the word *ordinary* mean?
   A. tricky
   B. evil
   C. normal
   D. weird

4. Which of the following people could be a witch?
   A. a teacher
   B. a police officer
   C. a nurse
   D. all of the above

5. Choose the sentence that best describes how a witch feels about children.
   A. She hates children.
   B. She loves children.
   C. She is afraid of children.
   D. She thinks children are funny.

The Witches **Sample Test**

Name_____ Date_____

Sample Test, Part 2

Directions: You are going to listen to a chapter from *The Witches* called "How To Recognize A Witch." Then you will answer two questions about the chapter.

Listen to the chapter twice. The first time you hear the chapter, only listen carefully. The second time you hear the chapter, take notes on what you hear. Then use your notes to help you answer the questions.

NOTES

The Witches   **Sample Test**

Name_____ Date_____

1. List the main characteristics of REAL WITCHES.

_____
_____
_____
_____
_____

2. Grandmama wanted to teach her grandson how to recognize a witch. Write about a time when someone in your family taught you something. In your story, remember to write
- who taught you
- what the person taught you
- why the person taught you that lesson

Check your writing for correct spelling, capitalization and punctuation.

_____
_____
_____
_____
_____
_____
_____
_____
_____

The Witches **Sample Test**

Name_____ Date_____

Sample Test, Part 3

Directions: You are going to read a chapter from *The Witches* called "The Meeting." Then you will answer a question about what you have read. You can look back in the chapter to help you answer the question.

1. Use details from the chapter to explain how the boy figured out that the women at the meeting were witches.

_____
_____
_____
_____
_____
_____
_____
_____
_____
_____
_____
_____
_____
_____

Appendix

Extension Activities Knowledge 1

Name _____ Date _____

Directions: List the characters in the boxes below.

Character # 1

Character # 2

Character # 3

Character # 4

Character # 5

Draw a picture of your favorite character.

Appendix 103

Extension Activities Knowledge 2

Name_____ Date_____

Directions: Answer the following questions.

What is the title of the story?
_____

Who is the author of the story?
_____

Who are the characters in the story?
_____
_____
_____
_____
_____

Where does the story take place?
_____
_____
_____
_____
_____

Extension Activities Comprehension 1

Name _____ Date _____

Directions: Explain how the main character felt at the beginning, middle, and end of the story. Illustrate your answers in the boxes.

BEGINNING _____ felt
_____ because
_____
_____
_____

MIDDLE _____ felt
_____ because
_____
_____
_____

END _____ felt
_____ because
_____
_____
_____

Appendix 105

Extension Activities **Comprehension 2**

Name_____ Date_____

Directions: Use the sequence words to retell the story in order.

First,_____
_____

Next,_____
_____

Then,_____
_____

After that,_____
_____

Soon,_____
_____

Finally,_____
_____

Extension Activities Application 1

Name_____ Date_____

Directions: Pretend you are making dinner for one of the characters. Illustrate what your dinner would look like on the plate below. Make a list of the ingredients on the lines below.

_____

_____

_____

_____

Appendix 107

Extension Activities Application 2

Name_____ Date_____

Directions: In the boxes below write three ways in which the character changed throughout the story.

Change #1

Change #2

Change #3

Extension Activities Analysis 1

Name_____ Date_____

Directions: Draw a picture of four of your favorite characters from the story in the circles below. Underneath each character's picture, write three words to describe the character.

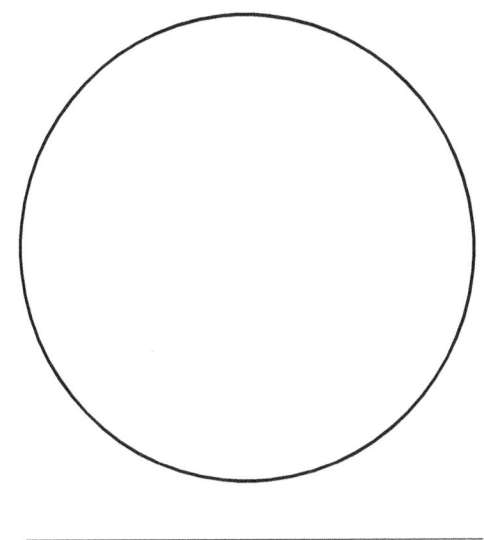
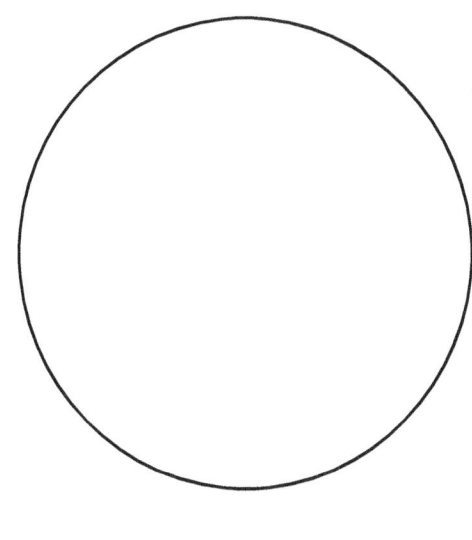

_____   _____

_____   _____

_____   _____

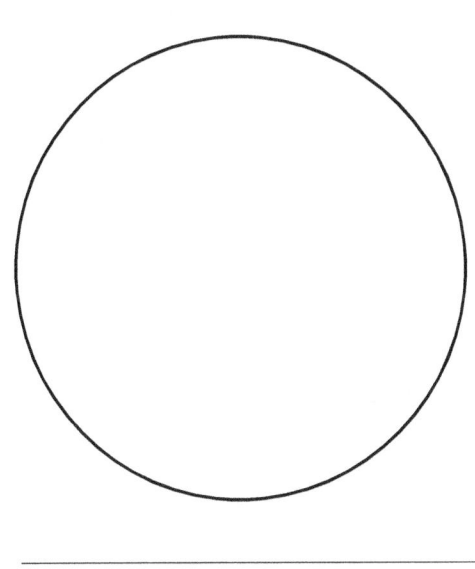
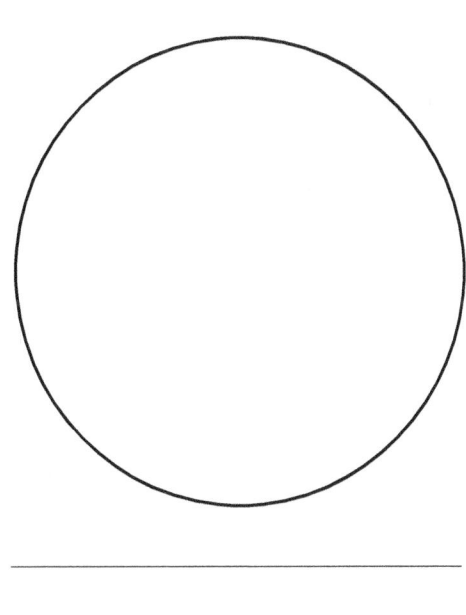

_____   _____

_____   _____

_____   _____

Appendix 109

Extension Activities Analysis 2

Name_____ Date_____

Directions: Use the Venn diagram below to compare and contrast two of the main characters from the story.

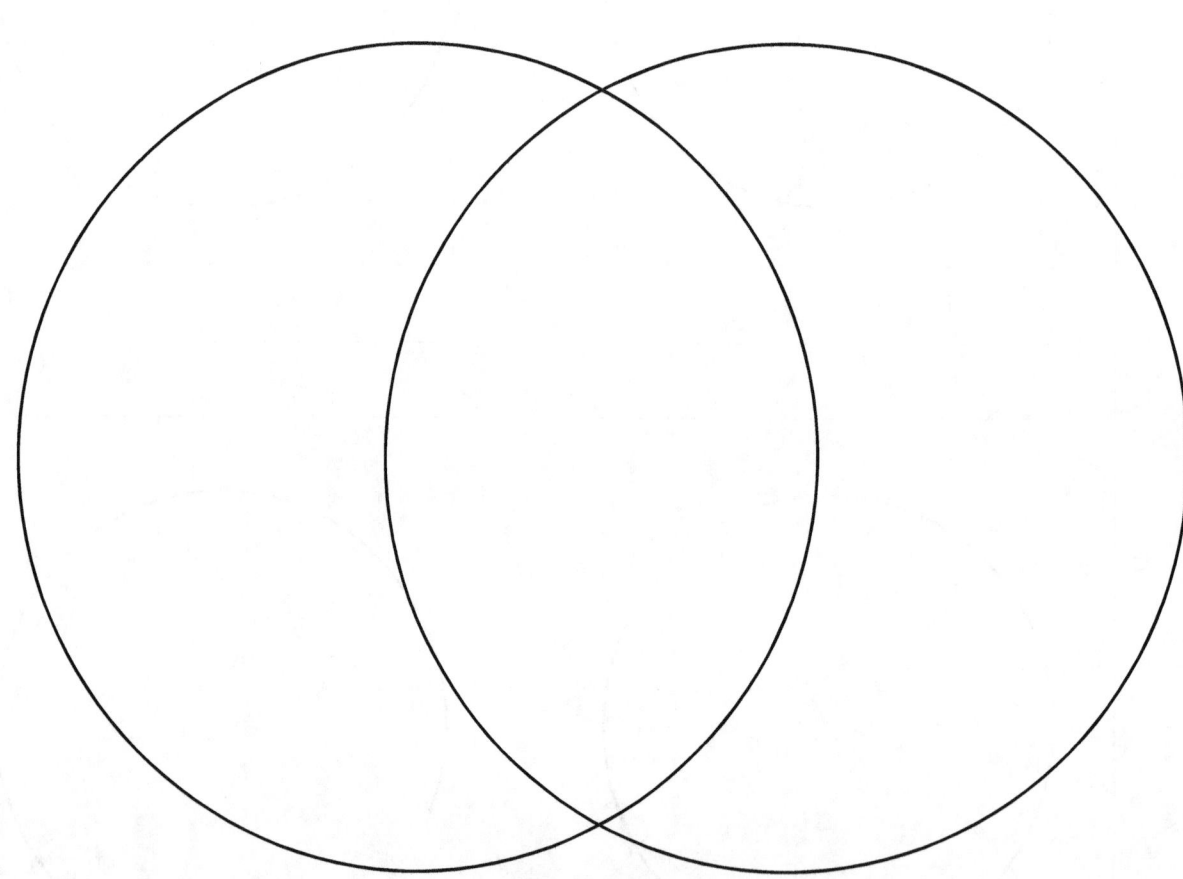

Extension Activities Synthesis 1

Name _____ Date _____

Directions: Create a new title for the story. Use at least three examples from the story to explain why you chose your title.

_____

Extension Activities Synthesis 2

Name_____ Date_____

Directions: Pretend you are the main character in the story. Write about your adventures in the diary below.

Day One

Date_____

Dear Diary,

_____
_____
_____
_____
_____
_____
_____

Day Two

Date_____

Dear Diary,

_____
_____
_____
_____
_____
_____
_____

Extension Activities **Evaluation 1**

Name_____ Date_____

Directions: Write a letter to a friend. Tell your friend whether or not he or she should read the book.

In your letter:
- Tell three things you liked about the story.
    or
- Tell three things that you didn't like about the story.

Dear_____,

_____

_____

_____

_____

_____

_____

_____

_____

_____

_____

_____

Your friend,

_____

Extension Activities Evaluation 2

Name_____ Date_____

Directions: Fill out the Book Critique below.

Name of Book _____

Author of Book _____

Classification (mark an X)

☐ Biography   ☐ How to   ☐ Fantasy

☐ Fable   ☐ Mystery   ☐ Science Fiction

Characters

_____

_____

What was the book about?

_____

_____

I would rate this book (circle one):

☆poor   ☆☆fair   ☆☆☆good   ☆☆☆☆excellent

I rated it _____ because _____

_____

Signature _____ Date _____